IMAGES
of England

ARNOLD

Aerial view of the Front Street and Cross Street area, *c.* 1950. The Croft is bottom left, with St Mary's Church top centre. The shopping centre has since been transformed and any empty space has been developed, mainly for housing.

IMAGES
of England

ARNOLD

Compiled by
M.W. Spick

TEMPUS

First published 2000
Copyright © M.W. Spick, 2000

Tempus Publishing Limited
The Mill, Brimscombe Port,
Stroud, Gloucestershire, GL5 2QG

ISBN 0 7524 1872 6

Typesetting and origination by
Tempus Publishing Limited
Printed in Great Britain by
Midway Clark Printing, Wiltshire

Cover illustration: The staff of the Allen Solly works, *c.* 1925.

Coat of arms of Arnold Urban District from 1948 to 1974, when it merged with Gedling Urban District. Its motto was *Alta Sententia,* meaning 'with high purpose'.

Contents

The area has been visited many times since the Norman Conquest by royalty using the adjacent Royal Hunting Park at Bestwood, but it was not until 1983 that the first official visit occurred when Princess Alexandra opened Moira House.

Introduction

The old parish of Arnold is situated three miles north of Nottingham on the road to the north. Although a Roman depot camp was established at Dorket Head, and the Saxons arrived in the sixth century and settled in what was then the great forest of Sherwood, Arnold is first recorded in the Domesday Survey of 1086 and was the headquarters of one of the nine divisions of the Forest. Being so isolated, its inhabitants did not have a wealthy life and poverty brought with it problems of survival and crime. In the 1770s the early Industrial Revolution brought many changes and by the 1840s life was so desperate that an appeal for government help was made and a Local Board was formed in 1854, lasting until 1894 when it was renamed the Parish Council.

I came to live in the area in 1951, and since then many changes have occurred, not least through the merger of Arnold with Gedling Urban District in 1974. It is this great number of changes (which are still continuing) which have made this record possible. In some respects the result of the changes has been sad, with the loss of many architectural treasures. The town's heritage of independence has disappeared, helped by the demise of the older population.

Today Arnold's main shopping centres are filled with inexpensive clothing, amusement arcades, charity shops, estate agents and banks. A successful market has been created but there is no cinema or bus station. It seems as though Arnold has become a dormitory town to the nearby City of Nottingham. Further changes are being planned, often behind closed doors, so it will be up to the future historian to record the end results.

In the thirteenth century, one of the nation's legends was created – Robin Hood (and his Merry Men). Despite continuing controversy over where he was born, lived and died, he still retains his identity in Sherwood Forest. This Edwardian view takes a light-hearted look at this local hero and Maid Marian; however, there may be some connection to the figure of legend, as one authority asserts that his headquarters were in this region near Jacob's Ladder and the Sherwood hospital.

Buildings of Specific Architectural or Historical Interest

Grade II*

Church of St Mary, Church Lane
Church of St Paul, Mansfield Road, Daybrook
Church of the Good Shepherd, Thackerays Lane, Woodthorpe

Grade II

42A Calverton Road
Boundary Wall, Church of St Mary, Church Lane
Arnold House, 15 Church Street
34 High Street
Bonington House, 79 High Street
Daybrook Almshouses, Mansfield Road
Gateway and Boundary Wall, Daybrook Almshouses, Mansfield Road
321 Mansfield Road and adjoining frame shop
Arnot Hill House, off Nottingham Road
Cockcliffe House and adjoining granary, off Ollerton Road
Ramsdale House and adjoining stable, Oxton Lane
Home Ales Brewery Offices and attached railings, Mansfield Road
Former J. & R. Morley hosiery factory, Mansfield Road
Hand shop at former Allen Solly factory, Brookfield Road
The Dairy, Dairy Farm, Mansfield Road
The Vale Hotel, Mansfield Road, Daybrook
Pub sign in front and to the west of the Vale Hotel, Mansfield Road, Daybrook
Oxclose Public House, Oxclose Lane
Coronation Buildings, 79-91 Mansfield Road, Daybrook
(issued April 1999 by the Gedling Urban District Council)

One
Mansfield Road from Daybrook to the Arch

Despite many changes some traditions still survive – this is an advertising postcard for a Daybrook laundry from the 1930s or '40s.

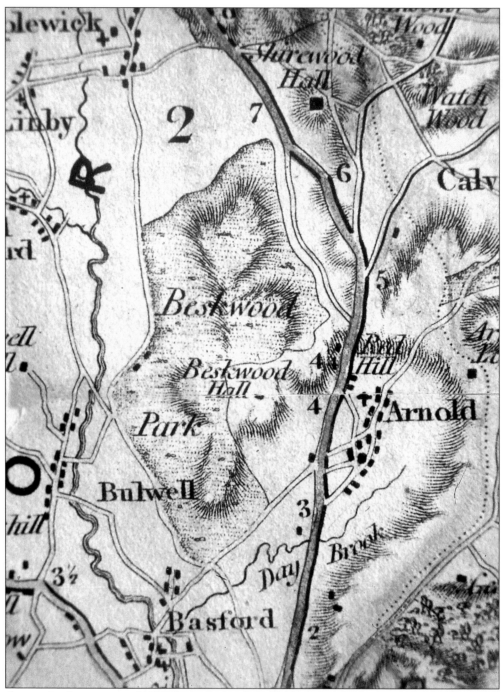

An extract from a map of 1775 showing the Arnold area. This map was printed on the eve of industrial growth in the area and clearly shows the isolation of the area, even though it is only a few miles from the town of Nottingham (off the south of the map). Bestwood Park on Arnold's western boundary was a Royal Forest from around 1105 until granted to Nell Gwynne by Charles II as revenue to support their offspring, who were created the Dukes of St Albans by Charles II.

Jacob's Ladder, Edwards Lane, Sherwood.

The Day Brook and Jacob's Ladder, *c.* 1930. The stream, originally known as 'Depe Brook', formed part of the parish's southern boundary, and was a delightful walk for many. The road in the background is Edwards Lane and today the Five Ways Inn stands on the right.

The Roxy Cinema was built in 1937, closed in 1960 and was converted into a bingo hall a year later. Its chief claim to fame was its involvement in 1951 in a local murder case. This picture dates from 1988; soon afterwards, after a number of years of neglect, the building was demolished and luxury flats were built on the site, named Valley Court.

Mansfield Road in the 1970s. On the eastern side there stood this property near the railway bridge. After use as a factory, the building was used as a Catholic church after emancipation. When the new Catholic church was built in 1929 the Christian Spiritualists replaced them here. At the side was the opening to Magdala Square – the most notorious dwellings in Arnold. The whole area has since been cleared for supermarkets.

Mansfield Road in 1955. In 1875 the railway arrived in Arnold. The house near the bridge (on the left) was the home of the stationmaster. In 1889 a suburban link with Nottingham joined the line on the left, but in the 1960s the line was closed, the bridge being taken down in 1966.

Mr Fox, the first stationmaster at Daybrook, in the 1870s.

Daybrook Station, Home Ales Skegness Trip, 1933.

With the coming of the railway, many people were given the freedom to travel further. Many local excursions were organized by the larger firms to Skegness and Mablethorpe – both nicknamed 'Nottingham by the Sea'. These employees of the Home Brewery about to set off for Skegness from Daybrook station in 1933.

GREAT NORTHERN RAILWAY.

NOTICE FOR FEBRUARY, 1876.

The Great Northern Train Service for January will, with the following exceptions, be continued **throughout February**, and until further notice :—

WEEK DAYS.

OPENING

OF THE FIRST SECTION OF THE

NEW NOTTINGHAMSHIRE LINE

FOR

PASSENGER TRAFFIC.

Trains will run as under :—

DOWN.		A.M.	A.M.	A.M.	P.M.	P.M.	P.M.	P.M.
Nottingham ... ... Dep.		7 30	9 50	11 20	12 40	3 50	5 8	6 20
Gedling and Carlton... ... ... „		7 40	10 0	11 30	12 50	4 0	5 18	6 30
Bestwood and Arnold ... ... „		7 47	10 7	11 37	12 57	4 7	5 25	6 37
New Basford (for Dob Pk. & Bulwell) Arr.		7 52	10 12	11 42	1 2	4 12	5 30	6 42

UP.		A.M.	A.M.	A.M.	P.M.	P.M.	P.M.	P.M.
New Basford (for Dob Pk. & Bulwell) Dep.		8 10	10 35	11 55	1 35	4 25	5 35	7 0
Bestwood and Arnold ... ... „		8 15	10 40	12 0 P.M.	1 40	4 30	5 40	7 5
Gedling and Carlton ... ... „		8 23	10 48	12 8	1 48	4 38	5 48	7 13
Nottingham... ... ... Arr.		8 35	11 0	12 20	2 0	4 50	6 0	7 25

Skegness and Firsby Branch.

The 6.45 a.m. Train from Skegness will run as under :—

						A.M.
Skegness	...	...	...	...	Dep.	6 38
Wainfleet	...	...	...	...	„	6 53
Firsby	...	...	...	...	Arr.	7 5

To stop at Cowbank, Croftbank, and Thorpe Culvert if required.

CITY AND SUBURBAN SERVICE.

The 4.5 p.m. Train, Moorgate Street to Enfield, will start at 4.3 p.m., and be 2 minutes earlier to King's Cross (G.N.)

The 4.32 p.m. Train, Broad Street to Enfield, and 5.25 p.m. Train, Enfield to Broad Street, will be discontinued.

New Trains will leave Broad Street at 5.32 p.m. for Enfield and intermediate Stations, and Enfield at 6.25 p.m. for Broad Street and intermediate Stations.

The 6.45 p.m. Train, King's Cross to East End, will be run to Highgate only.

SUNDAYS.
West Riding District.

The 6.50 p.m. Train, Shipley to Bradford, will be 10 minutes earlier throughout.
The 8. 0 p.m. Train, Kirkgate to Bradford, will be 10 minutes later throughout.
The 8.25 p.m. Train, Ardsley to Bradford, will be 10 minutes later throughout.
The 8.50 p.m. Train, Shipley to Bradford, will be 15 minutes later throughout.

KING'S CROSS STATION,
27th January, 1876.

HENRY OAKLEY,
General Manager.

Please attach this Notice to the January Time Books and Bills.

The first timetable for the Nottinghamshire line, February 1876.

14

Mansfield Road in the early 1970s. This row of dwellings stood at the side of the railway entrance on the left, and soon after the loss of the railway they disappeared for more superstores.

Miss Barrow's shop at the station entrance, early 1970s. Beattie (left) received the Maundy money in 1984 and a plaque has been installed in St Paul's church to commemorate her life-long work in the community. She died in 1993 aged 100 years.

I. & R. Morley's factory was opened in 1885 and closed in 1963, and is seen here before the Second World War. It was one of several companies that moved into Arnold at this time and the factory is now a listed building. One mystery remains: why was it named I. & R. Morley when the founder brothers were John and Richard? At the time of the factory's closure, Fine Wires was established in the building on the right, but the property is now vacant and a £5 million proposal to convert the premises into luxury flats has been announced.

A group of I. & R. Morley's directors in 1938.

Near I. & R. Morley's factory there was originally this filling station, owned by Mr Dove. It was replaced by a number of shops in the mid-1930s.

THE
DAYBROOK SOAP Co.,
LIMITED,
DAYBROOK, NOTTS.

Makers of the celebrated 'Lawreate' Soaps,

AND OF

Every class of household and Toilet Soap.

EVERY ONE SHOULD TRY the CLEANSER SOAP

The Household Wonder Worker.

The soap-making industry in Daybrook is now just a memory.

Jacoby's Factory, 1885. It was opened in 1884. A disastrous fire caused over £20,000 worth of damage in 1913 and in 1939 a second conflagration caused a loss of £100,000. The chimney was a noted landmark until 1951, but all that remains today are the two lowest floors.

Daybrook Square in 1934. The 'square' is clearly visible and the road opposite is Sherbrook Road. The tall building at the top marked what was then the parish boundary. Note the white roof, which belonged to a 'standing room gentlemen's urinal'.

In 1936 the family business of W.E. Berry was established and in 1998 it became the new Post Office for Daybrook.

Daybrook Square, February 1959. On the left are the buildings used by the Post Office which opened in March 1893 and closed seventy years later. The public house in the centre is the Grove Hotel, which was opened in 1860 and today is a 'real ale' house.

Oxclose Lane is the main thoroughfare into Arnold from the west. These two views provide a sharp contrast between 1922, when it really was a country lane, and today's dual carriageway.

Sunrise Hill. Above is a rural scene, surprisingly dating from as late as 1950. The urgent need to solve the social problems caused by poor housing has resulted in the construction of the estate shown below by 1987. The stands of trees on the horizon now provide the only reference point between the two views.

Bulwell Fields, to the rear of White Hart Farm, *c*. 1918. In the nineteenth century, the destitute would travel to the nearby regional workhouse at Bulwell, which was opened in 1836 and is now the Highbury Hospital. In the background is the spire of the cemetery chapel.

Roundwood Road, seen here in the 1970s, is a typical example of the housing programme initiated after the Second World War.

Coronation Buildings, Mansfield Road, were built in 1937 and in January 1999 were graded as listed buildings. They are seen here in 1993.

An Edwardian postcard view of the cottages which stood on the site of Coronation Buildings until the mid-1930s.

The Home Brewery was founded by J. Robinson, first in Church Street, then Cross Street, before settling down on this seventeen-acre site at Mansfield Road. This photograph shows the frontage until the mid-1930s when more modern architecture was completed, complemented by a tower that was finished after the Second World War. In 1877 it was known as John Robinson Brewery, producing fifty barrels a week. The Killingsley Spirits works were obtained in 1926 and by 1987 when Newcastle & Brown bought it, it controlled a wide range of assets.

The highlight of the workers' year was the annual trip to the coast. This one was in 1936, to Scarborough.

The Wells at Daybrook

There was a time, many generations ago, when breweries were frequently sited near to the barley fields and the hop fields. Water was a secondary consideration. Nowadays the importance of a good water supply is more generally recognised and many a famous beer is regarded as largely indebted to the outstanding qualities of its local water.

Daybrook is, as we mentioned earlier, exceptionally well situated in the matter of water supply. The Brewery itself rests on a bed of fine sandstone running to a depth of over 300 feet. Beneath this sandstone are huge natural reservoirs of the purest water.

REST WATER LEVEL **53** FT.

BUNTER PEBBLE BEDS
Coarse grained brownish red false bedded sandstones with well worn pebbles

105 FT.

150 FT.

LOWER MOTTLED SANDSTONE
Fine grained sandstones with local marl bands

250 FT.

PERMIAN BEDS
Lower Magnesian limestone overlying lower Permian marl

320 FT.

COAL MEASURES
Shales with thin sandstones and coal seams

435 FT.

An important asset for the brewery was the quality of water used for brewing, and this plan shows the depths the firm was willing to go to obtain it.

Large cellars were also built for storing purposes. Their fate is unknown, since the site was completely destroyed except for the main premises on Mansfield Road.

The Mansfield Road was from olden times the main route to the North, yet it is difficult to appreciate this in this photograph taken in 1925. It became the Mansfield Road when the Turnpike Halts were created in 1787. The building is the Daybrook Laundry, founded in 1875 by Samuel Robinson. In 1904 it became a Limited Company and by 1912 over 500 people were employed. Despite severe competition from electrical devices, the business continues and today is served by twenty-two vans which between them cover over 350,000 miles a year.

The old premises of the Daybrook Laundry illuminated in the 1930s.

The Daybrook Laundry (left) in 1999, with the Old Spot inn beside it. The inn is known from records since 1784; at the present time a sixty-two bedroom hotel is being added to it. The view is taken from the new Sir John Robinson Way, created through the old Brewery site.

A rare view of St Paul's church, Redhill, and nearby buildings in the 1930s, taken from the top of the brewery tower. The church was the gift of the Seely family in response to a need generated as the town developed southwards. It was built between 1895 and 1897 and contains a magnificent reredos which is now showing signs of wear. The row of houses in front were a memorial home erected in memory of Sandford Robinson in 1899.

A sketch of the interior of St Paul's in 1895, which appeared in the local newspaper of the time.

From 1890 the area was served by missionary helpers in this vehicle until the first building at St Paul's (now the annexe at the rear) was completed and first used.

ST. PAUL'S, DAYBROOK.
SUNDAY SCHOOL SPORTS, 1929.

Two contrasting events at St Paul's church. To the left are two views of the Sunday school sports day in 1929 which was held on the Home Farm in Oxclose Lane. Below is the funeral procession for Mrs Seely in the second decade of the twentieth century. Later a canopied memorial to her was placed in the church, near the altar.

Salop Street was the home of a local celebrity, known as 'Bronno'. The house on the left corner, which had one of the town's two dovecotes in its roof, was reputedly where Dick Turpin stayed on his famous ride to York. Today there is a new health centre on the corner and small businesses and an ambulance station are situated nearby.

A medal commemorating the visit of King George V and Queen Mary to Arnold, 24 June 1914.

Mansfield Road between Salop Street and the White Hart, *c.* 1965. This stretch of the road was known as Sloethorn before the importance of the site meant that the dilapidated houses shown here were pulled down for modern building. The first shop was the headquarters of the Pioneer Speed King, who died in January 2000 aged ninety-five.

In 1909 Matilda Lambert and her three children were murdered in Arnold by her partner, Samuel Atherley. He was found guilty and was hanged at Bagthorpe Prison in Sherwood. These illustrations of the funeral cortege are an early example of actual photographs being used in newspapers. In an 'information background' section, the article states that 8,000 people reside here and that the area has produced many well-known cricketers!

The junction of Oxclose Lane and Mansfield Road in 1920, before the road was widened. In the late eighteenth century it was described as a wild, bleak area, but in 1787 the Mansfield Road was made into a turnpike. There were two toll gates – one at Woodthorpe, the other here. However, a dispute arose and it was later moved to Daybrook Square. The road was freed of tolls ninety years later.

The same area in the early 1980s – there has been a complete transformation.

The White Hart Inn, seen on the right in this photograph, can be traced back to 1765. This view is of an unknown parade, possibly related to the First World War as soldiers feature prominently in the scene. The inn has since been taken over and rebuilt behind the original, and is known as the Beefeater. Also situated behind was Spencers Farm and the old entrance to Bestwood Lodge.

Many of the buildings opposite the White Hart were demolished for road widening, but the large white building known as the Dolls Factory was preserved and now houses the local Social Services department.

Goodwood House from Mansfield Road. In 1883 Mr Acton won a large sum of money at the races, and this house was built with his windfall.

Bestwood Park used to house a well-known cricket ground, used by (among others) the Redhill Baptist Football Club. Their team for the 1920/21 season is photographed on the 'Pond' recreation ground, in front of the entrance to Bestwood Lodge.

The Cemetery, Redhill, was opened in 1879 on land given by the Duke of St Albans. It has since been extended a number of times and today covers over twenty-five acres and over 25,000 people have been interred here. The cemetery has been controlled by the Council since 1916 and until recently any enquiry was answered by the Council's Recreation Department!

The final resting place of the Robinson family.

In February 1967 the spire of the cemetery chapel was destroyed by lightning. In its restoration it was replaced by a small tower and the public clock from the Ebenezer Church on Front Street was installed.

These old cottages on the east side of Mansfield Road, dating from around 1825, were demolished in the 1950s.

This row of dwellings opposite was preserved. They are seen here in around 1930.

A motor accident at the Redhill Road junction, 1955. The old village grew in this area from around 1800 and the post office was established on the corner of Mansfield Road from 1902. Between 1880 and 1882 postal business was transacted at the Guide House, then known as Five Mile House. Increasing traffic coming from the north made the area very hazardous, and the shops were demolished to be replaced by a bungalow. The frontage was preserved at the Longsdale Craft Centre at Ravenswood.

Easom's chippy at Redhill in 1970, one of many to disappear. It is believed to have been the oldest in the area, which in 1946 boasted twenty-six such businesses. Note the prices in 1970: 1s 4d for cod and 9d for chips. Today, prices are £2.40 for fish and 90p for chips – an increase of 25-30 times.

The village contained this row of cottages nicknamed 'The Barracks', so called because it is said that recruits were assembled here prior to military training.

A general view of the village looking north in 1930. Most of the property on the left has disappeared but the two pubs, the Ram (begun in 1789) and the Wagon and Horses (behind the Ram), are still extant.

Arnold Orphanage was erected in 1887. It is seen here shortly before it closed in the early 1920s.

Redhill School and Centre was built on the site of the orphanage in 1948 and at its side the new post office was opened in 1979. This area was also known as Derrymount, which may have been named during the Irish war around 1690.

The Guide House at Redhill, *c.* 1958. The origins of the building could be traced back to 1562 and its seventeenth-century occupants were often in trouble for illegal brewing. Also in this period there are tales of assignations between Charles II and Nell Gwynne, but unfortunately these are not substantiated. Recently the house and lands were cleared for a new housing estate. During the changeover a plaque was unearthed with the inscription on it, reading: 'L.R.E. 1716'.

This row of cottages escaped destruction when the Guide House disappeared, but they have been modernized internally. They are seen here in 1968.

Mansfield Road, Redhill, 1930. Nestling at the foot of the hill, a thriving business was created to cater for passengers in carriages, then a relatively new form of transport, at the beginning of the nineteenth century. So successful were they that there were seven taverns to cater for their needs, but many have now vanished.

Red Hill Motts

An Edwardian view of Red Hill, the steep slope from which the hamlet at the bottom takes its name.

The Redhill Arch was first recorded in 1218. In 1815 the unemployed were set to work lowering the road and building a large solid bridge, seen here in 1865, as an access into Bestwood. Since that time three more bridges have replaced it.

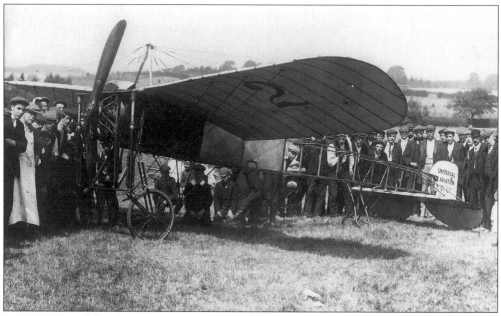

In 1911 the *Daily Mail* 'Round Britain Air Race' took place and one plane had to land near the Arch, attracting thousands of viewers. The pilot took off the next morning after breakfast at the Wagon and Horses.

Two
The Nottingham Road and Gedling Road Areas

An aerial view of Daybrook, c. 1960. At this time the area was on the verge of wholesale development; the land leading to the Plains Road at the top of the picture (the eastern boundary of the parish) was still open land.

This page shows two historical landmarks at the beginning of Nottingham Road. Above is Cottage Row, built to house some of the 1,000 workers at the Arnold Mill. When the mill closed, Cottage Row was turned into fifteen houses. A well-known character who lived here was 'Catty Nan'. The row was demolished (along with an eighteenth-century baking oven and cave) to make way for a lorry park.

The Meadow School was built in 1790 by the mill manager. It was later used for a variety of purposes, including as a Chartist headquarters, a school where the sixteen-year-old teacher dealt with over 100 pupils, and as a council yard until its demolition in 1965.

Arnold fire station was built in 1935 and is seen here in the mid-sixties. It was later demolished to make way for newer premises. Today it is manned by four crewmen on call by day and nine crewmen at night.

The Arnold fire brigade in 1921.

Arnot Hill House had strong associations with the Mill from 1791 to 1811 and, after the Mill closed, became a private residence. In 1914 the Council decided to acquire it for its civic headquarters but although it was purchased by the Council it remained unoccupied because of the First World War, during which it became an auxiliary hospital. After the war the Council reverted to its original intention and used the house until the new civic centre was built at the side of it.

An outing for members of Arnold Urban District Council to Wickstead Park in August 1932.

The new civic centre was opened in 1985 by Princess Anne (above) who then made a tour of the premises. The picture below shows the centre in 1997.

The lake in Arnot Hill Park, 1974. It has always been a Mecca for children of all ages, despite the rather curiously worded notice.

The R.P. Bonington statue erected in the foyer of the civic centre. R.P. Bonington, Arnold's most famous celebrity, was born on High Street in 1802 and died at the early age of twenty-six. He was considered to be one of the architects of the 'English School'. In 1912 a canopied statue was erected outside the School of Art in Nottingham, but the weather was unkind to the material and so it was dismantled and stored in Nottingham Castle Museum, until it emerged in 1992 at the civic centre.

These two views show the ceremonies for bestowing the Freedom of the Borough on the local regiment, the Sherwood Foresters, in October 1977.

A striking example of change from a rural landscape to residential use can be judged by this painting of Sandfield Road. The picture was painted in 1911 by Sybil Fisher. The cottage, believed to be of seventeenth-century origin, still stands. The road was known as early as the 1780s.

Another view, this time of Greendale Road leading to the Moor. The children are playing on the old discontinued railway line, just before the redevelopment of the area.

The Arrow public house was built to serve the increasing needs of the area in 1969 but within a few years its distinctive architecture fell out of favour and a more elegant structure was erected to replace it. The old building is seen here in 1993.

May Day celebrations were held annually in Arnot Hill Park. This shows the celebrations in the mid-1920s.

A demonstration in Nottingham Road in the 1970s, a time when frustration in the workplace was widespread. Later the gates on the right were closed as a wider entrance was developed.

In 1929 the 'Bottom Rec' was established and the assembly point for the annual event of the year – the Whit Tuesday parade – was transferred from the Flower Field on Worrall Avenue. This is the parade in 1950.

The Whit Parade was the event of the year, when each Sunday School paraded down to the Worrall Field (and since 1929 to the 'Bottom Rec.'). This view probably dates from the years of the First World War, given the presence of soldiers in the crowd.

By the 1970s motor floats were used in the parade. Many of the drays had a 'topical' theme as this one, participating in the 1971 event, shows.

Another view of a decorated lorry waiting to be judged (Note the spelling mistakes!).

Even the weather of 1975 did not deter the enthusiasm.

Amid all the excitement and confusion, it has always been a priority to make the Whit Parade a special event for the children, as shown here in 1968.

Children from the Congregational Church Sunday school taking part in the 1936 Whit Parade on St Albans Road.

By the late 1970s the parades were losing their appeal. Partly because of the increasing volume of traffic the event was transferred to the King George Playing Fields and finally ended in 1977. This is the Parade for 1976. Attempts by folk groups continued for a few more years and plans are in hand to revive it in 2000.

After the sale of the Home Brewery site on Nottingham Road, big changes were soon evident. This property was the first to be erased.

More demolition was to follow. The Edwardian houses above were demolished in 1997 and the houses below were also quickly eliminated. The cottage in between was the only one marked on the Enclosure map of 1789.

The Apollo Works suffered the same fate. Erected in 1923, at the height of its production it was producing over 2 million bottles of water per week. It is shown here in 1997, shortly before demolition.

An aerial view of the Apollo Works, along with Folly Yard (so named after the failure of the Arnold Mill). They were both demolished to make way for a new road, Sir John Robinson's Way.

In 1998 the new Sainsbury's was opened and shortly afterwards the original Brewery offices were taken over by the County Council. Other businesses now filling the site include a Royal Mail sorting office, a restaurant, a car sales emporium and some private houses.

In the early 1960s many people contributed to funds, under the leadership of Mr H. Cave, to erect an old people's centre opposite Sainsbury's.

Nottingham Road. This row of houses was built as workrooms for the knitters. The worker used the top-floor rooms and stored the finished work in the manager's house, which protruded onto the edge of the road.

Nottingham Road once again, but looking in the opposite direction to the photograph above. The land on the left is clearly still undeveloped. The row of trees at the rear is the location of Arnot Hill Road. The crowd is assembling for a Whit Parade, probably before the First World War.

The Greyhound Inn was known as early as 1832. This view dates from the early years of the twentieth century; the houses beyond the pub have since gone.

Nottingham Road, *c.* 1920. The Carnegie Library, opened in 1906, is on the right in the middle distance and the St Alban's Theatre or Picturedrome is on the far right. The entrance to Arnot Hill Road was formed between them.

The junction of Church Drive with St. Alban's Road. Taken in the early twentieth century, this view shows the orchard which once stood there. When it was removed a large space was left and has never been occupied. The crowds are preparing for a Whit Parade.

Until 1876, St Alban's Road was a main thoroughfare to Mansfield Road known as Broadmere Lane. All of these houses were later swept away and their place taken by modern dwellings.

This row of cottages, along with one behind it, Holt's Row, figured in the evidence of the Enquiry of 1853 which examined the living conditions and the state of the village at that time. This view dates from 1959.

Co-op Corner was built in 1904. After ceasing to house the Co-op, it was sold and used as a furniture and bedding store until it was converted into new public house called The Ernehale, which opened in October 1999.

The Drill Hall on Arnot Hill Road was opened in 1914 for recruiting purposes, but is now the home of small businesses.

The Round House in Hallams Lane, 1924. This unusual building was near the site of the old pinfold, but was demolished in 1937.

The village of Arnold was concentrated along both sides of the main street and it is difficult to realize how close the open fields just behind were – they were the beginning of the walks which gave so much pleasure. On the right is the path from Arnot Hill Road which led to the 'Moor', portrayed in a painting dating from 1932. It is now the site of Castleton Avenue. The picture below shows a stile on a path near Kingswell Farm, leading to the 'Rookery'. This photograph taken in 1925 appears to include some mysterious ghosts at the stile....

Anthony Higginbottom (1842-1895) was the first headmaster of the British School which stood on the site of the present market. He was also an eminent architect, and lived in the cottage at 19 Hallams Lane, pictured below in 1960.

ON, BESTWOOD, PAR

CRICKET. GROUN

During the twentieth century the most popular location for socializing was the 'local', but sport, particularly football played by religious and other organizations, was enjoyed on the recreation grounds. Arnold had four of these: The 'Top Rec' (north of the parish church), the 'Bottom Rec' already mentioned, the 'Pond' near St Albans Road (flooding being a frequent deterrent here) and the cricket ground in Bestwood Park, pictured here.

The White Star FC, the forerunner of St Mary's team and Arnold Town, in the early part of the twentieth century.

Memories were often recalled when older sportsmen met, and this group of 1920s sportsmen, meeting up in the 1970s, were no exception.

St Mary's Church Committee pictured at Calverton Road School after a victory in the early 1950s. From left to right, back row: -?-, ? Eddyshaw, R. Hinson, J. Wharton, C. Moore, C. Moore. Front row: ? Ridge, S. Gray, M. Evans, J. Kirk (secretary), W. Parr (chairman), T. Greg.

Arnold St Mary's FC, successors to the White Star club pictured on p. 70, after winning the Notts. Senior Cup, probably at some time during the 1960s. From left to right, back row: B. Molynex, N. Gough, E. Ironmonger, N. Simpson, D. Parr (Captain), J. Anthony, G. Gregory (Trainer). Front row: J. Moore, R. Leverton, B. Coombe, Terry Gray (mascot), C. Colindridge, P. Williams. In an earlier era of the club's history, in 1935, one J. Seedhouse scored 10 of the 17 goals scored – both figures being a record for local matches.

Sport in Arnold received a boost when the playing fields on Gedling Road were donated by the Home Brewery. This is the Arnold women's football team of 1921, who raised thousands of pounds to help distressed families.

Arnold FC's moment of fame came in 1967 when Bristol Rovers played here, but lost 3-0. This is the victorious local team. From left to right, back row: Ray Knight, Jack Davis, Dave Smith, Terry Straw, John Anthony, Vince Howard. Front row: Barry Dunn, John Moore, Joe Boucher, Bobby Tait, John Langford, Peter Burton.

Although not as popular as football, cricket nevertheless had a sizeable following from very early times, for as early as 1853 an all Arnold team played an all England team, causing great excitement. This picture shows the cricket team for the 1885 season, which played on the Bestwood pitch. Note the formal attire and the enormous bat!

Arnold cricket team in the 1950s.

Opposite the King George Playing Fields is the beginning of Gedling Road. The illustration above shows the buildings which were present in 1956; the British School is on the left. Fifty years later it has been transformed into the market place, seen below in 1999. A market place had been proposed as early as 1868, but it never materialized.

Just behind Gedling Road was another large factory – Allen Solly's, seen here in 1960. The firm came to Arnold in the eighteenth century but, although the building remains, the company suffered the fate of many other local enterprises and closed in 1975.

OPENING FREE LIBRARY ARNOLD NOTTS.

The opening ceremony for the Free Library on Nottingham Road, 1906.

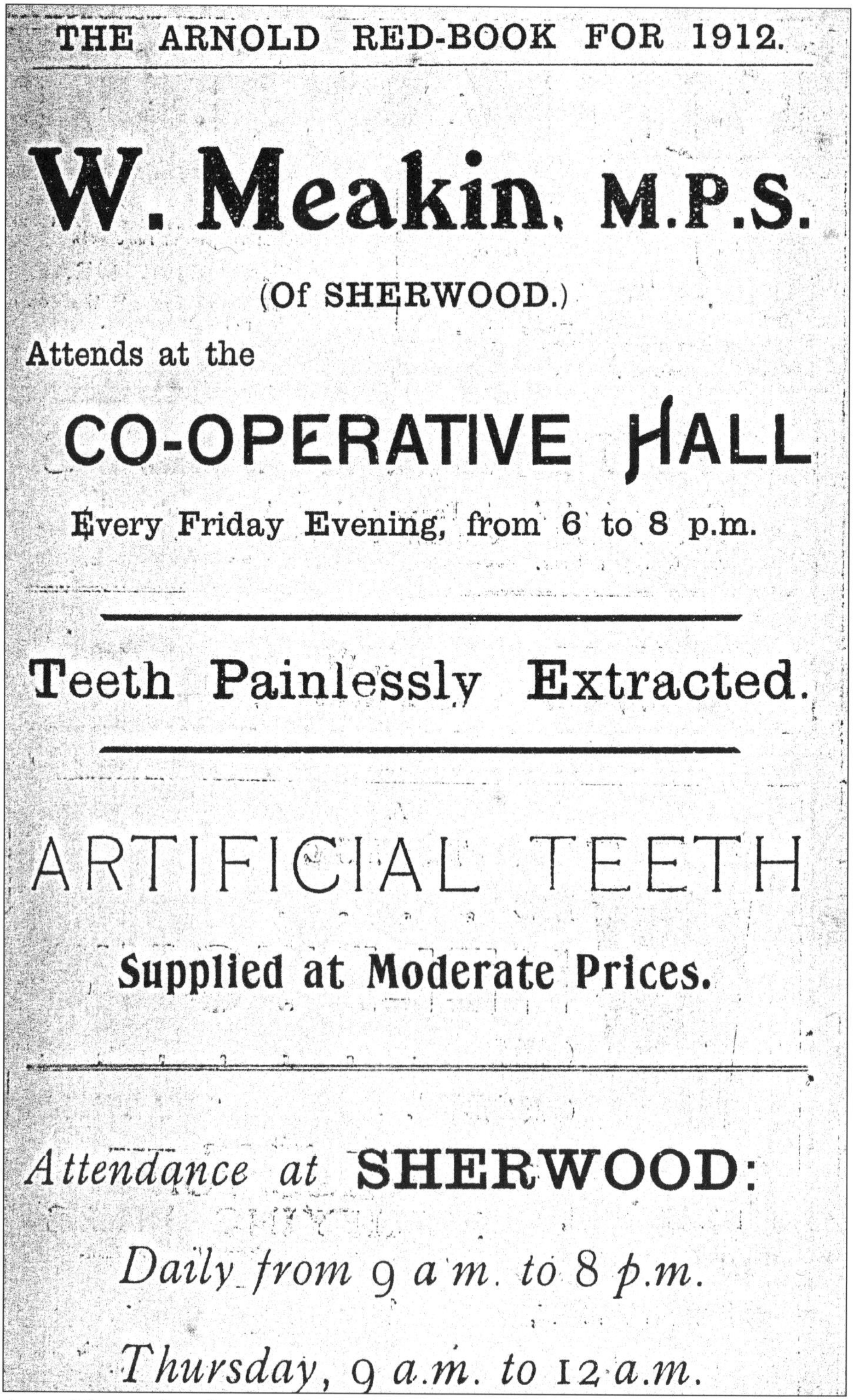

THE ARNOLD RED-BOOK FOR 1912.
W. Meakin, M.P.S.
(Of SHERWOOD.)
Attends at the
CO-OPERATIVE HALL
Every Friday Evening, from 6 to 8 p.m.
Teeth Painlessly Extracted.
ARTIFICIAL TEETH
Supplied at Moderate Prices.
Attendance at SHERWOOD:
Daily from 9 a.m. to 8 p.m.
Thursday, 9 a.m. to 12 a.m.
A painful reminder of an everyday health problem: a dentist's advertisement from 1912.

Three
The High Street Area

An early view of the junction of Nottingham Road, High Street (on the left) and Front Street.

A panoramic view of the High Street and Front Street junction, *c.* 1930. Front Street is on the right.

The east side of the High Street in 1999.

Front Street in 1999. The street has now been pedestrianized, but most of the shops retain their former appearance, at least above the ground floor. The road was re-paved in co-operation with Sainsbury's.

The Primitive Methodist church in the High Street, c. 1951. The church was later demolished for road widening purposes. It served as the mission church for the area in 1822 and amalgamated with the Front Street church in 1967.

Brailsford's shop, seen here in 1958, was also demolished. More popularly known as the town's pawnshop, it worked overtime in the lean years and it featured in many distressing tales of people striving to make ends meet.

Number 34 High Street, built between 1725 and 1740, is a classic example of quality restoration.

Bonington House, named after Arnold's most famous resident. It has been occupied since 1909 by the local Labour Party, who bought it, the grounds and two adjacent cottages for £700, and has recently been modernized.

One of the early victims to fall as the large businesses arrived was Arnold Dairies. The building stood derelict for a while after the business closed, but it was later demolished and a funeral parlour now stands on the site.

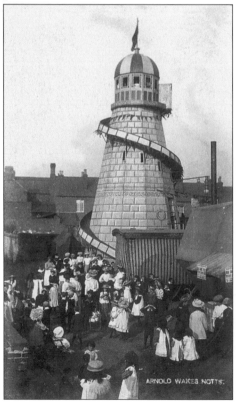

The highlight for many in Arnold were the September Wakes. The general opinion is that their origins lie in a religious ceremony practised by Catholics until 1408. In 1810 it was suggested that the Wakes should be moved to the week before the Nottingham Goose Fair, and this remained a point of debate until the 1830s. In 1859 it was reported that the people's morals and behaviour at the event had improved in recent years. Many difficulties were overcome, but by 1963 the Wakes were doomed. A health centre, mobility unit, car park and public toilets now occupy the area used for the event.

In the 1870s, the Salvation Army visited Arnold, but their visit was not a success. For many years the Salvation Army combined Arnold with Basford, but in October 1995 it established a permanent meeting house on High Street. This photograph shows the great interest shown by the local population on the opening day, 21 October 1995.

Because of the parallel layout of Front and High Street, any development would involve many properties on both roads. These houses on High Street, pictured in 1959, were some of the first to go, to make way for a car park.

The High Street schools in the early 1980s. Built as a result of the Education Acts in the late nineteenth century, they were replaced recently. A new police station and small business premises now occupy the area. College Street, which runs between the schools, was closed off in 1967.

York Terrace, more popularly known as Blackbird Row, in 1963. These houses have also disappeared for ever.

One of the many rows of houses between Front Street and High Street, Kelk's Yard was inevitably doomed as the area was changing. It was replaced by the new library, swimming pool and theatre, which were erected in 1981/82.

The junction between the High Street and Cross Street was always known as Four Lane Ends. Much of the property has been cleared in the redevelopment of the area.

Cross Street is an important thoroughfare to the Mansfield Road from the original village. This view shows some typical houses of the nineteenth century (in one of which lived the Arnold eccentric Tommy Annibal).

Even in the nineteenth century land for housing was at a premium, just as it is at now. This is well illustrated in this view of the tiny Bumblebee Cottage which stood opposite the Baptist church, just below the houses shown above.

Four
The Front Street Area

An Edwardian view of Front Street, showing the Carnegie Library on the right.

An aerial view of central Arnold taken in 1972. Nottingham Road comes in from the bottom left-hand corner and splits into High Street, to the left, and Front Street, to the right. It does not show the many alterations which have affected the area in recent years.

Many changes have been made over the last few years and some of the first shops to vanish were these at the junction of High Street and Front Street. The area was transformed and is now known as the Green.

Front Street in the 1950s.

The southern end of Front Street, *c.* 1930. Front Street had been known as Town Street, Main Street and Church Street before the town settled on Front Street in 1876.

One of the best-known views in Arnold, showing Packer's Corner in Edwardian times. Halfway along was the police station, built in 1861, which boasted two brick cells.

The British Schools, 1960. They were opened in 1868 and demolished over a hundred years later to make room for the market place.

The beginning of Gedling Road today, with the market on the right. The establishment of a market was proposed as long ago as 1868 but did not come to fruition for over a century. A sign – something of a misnomer – at the corner of Coppice Road advertised the non-existent Arnold Market for many years.

Mr S. Spencer, a popular headmaster of the British Schools.

This open space was renamed the Square during the many changes which have taken place recently; it is seen here in 1989. This clock originally stood outside Mount Street bus station and was relocated here for a short period, but was soon a target for mindless vandalism.

EBENEZER CHAPEL. ARNOLD, NOTTS

The Methodist Church arrived in the district as early as 1800 and the building above was erected in 1865 with the public clock installed one year later. The three Methodist movements were joined together in 1932 but it was not until 1967 that they merged to occupy one church, seen below. The new church was built on the site of the old chapel, which was demolished in 1966. The original chapel was also known as the Ebenezer, originally meaning 'temple of stone'.

METHODIST CHURCH, ARNOLD, NOTTINGHAM

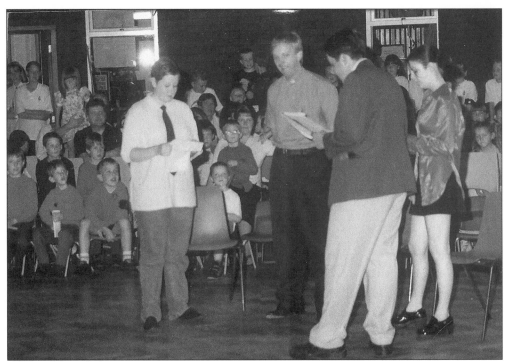

Despite the decline in church attendances, many activities of all kinds still take place in and around churches. This gathering was photographed recently at the 'Church in the Market Place' (also nicknamed the 'Pepperpot').

One of the most persistent problems facing Arnold's main thoroughfare is the constant threat of flooding. By a strange irony of circumstances the same day as the new pedestrianized part of Front Street was officially opened, 18 July 1975, a severe rainstorm caused the problem to emerge again. The area is now known as the 'Lake District'.

Suttons Farm at the corner of Worrall Avenue, shortly before it was demolished to make way for new shops in 1992. Further along Worrall Avenue on the right is the post office. Arnold post office was officially opened as a receiving house on Front Street in 1844. It moved to No. 97 in 1881 and then to Worrall Avenue in 1936. Opposite it, a new feature was created called Post Office Square. The owners of the first property to be sold – used as a hairdressing salon – placed a plaque on the wall, but owing to uncertainty the development project was abandoned.

Four young men out for an evening stroll in 1928. Only partial names are known, from left to right: ? Sutton, A. Rowbottom, -?-, ? Sutton. Can anyone identify them more precisely?

CHESTNUT HOUSE BOARDING ACADEMY

Chestnut House Boarding Academy was a source of pride for the local education board. It was run by Miss Robinson for many years before it eventually closed.

Miss Robinson's class at Chestnut House dressed in costume, early twentieth century.

This building once housed the New Inn, hence the advertisements on the walls for bottled ales and Apollo table waters. In 1932 it closed and later became Rogers' cycle shop.

The Croft from Front Street, 1930. Mrs Pavier's shop is on the left and the Horse and Jockey – known in 1797 – is on the right.

Front Street in 1930. This shows the Empress Cinema and Dance Hall, which opened in 1915, on the right. With the decline of the cinema, the building became Woolworths, then Boots, before closing. The small building next to it is Rowbottoms the butchers and next to that is the Cross Keys, built in 1787. The Local Board met here in 1853. In 1998 it was redecorated and renamed The Famous Old Keys.

The oldest known photograph of anywhere in Arnold is this one of a farm at the corner of Ravenswood Road, next to the Cross Keys. It was taken in 1856.

The old council offices on the east side of Front Street, 1957. The new police station is on the right and next to it is Tom Turner's annexe. The upper storey the latter was used by the Council as offices up until 1919.

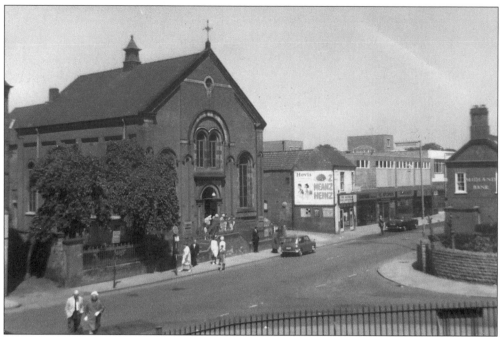

The Baptist church, Front Street. Constructed in 1840, it served the faithful until 1958 when it was sold and moved to the Killisick Estate. In this picture the congregation is leaving after the final service held in the church.

The old Baptist church was replaced by this new building, complete with floodlighting, as seen here. However, its out-of-the way site had a downward effect on attendances.

This Co-op store replaced the old Baptist church, but problems arose when the cemetery alongside came to be closed. The issue was resolved when the remains buried in the cemetery were reinterred beneath the brick memorial shown below. A new right of way was also established, seen on the left in the lower picture.

A favourite with people of all ages was Kitty, seen here with her workmate Mr Bleazard. She was the last animal employed by the Council, after which she retired, to live to a good age.

A very well-known local personality, Police Inspector W. ('Billy') Bishop (1865-1959). A native of Carlton on Trent, he joined the force in 1885, and was stationed in the area temporaraily before settling down in Arnold. He retired in 1921 and was presented with a watch and cheque, this being the first such presentation in the area. When he died he was believed to be one of the oldest pensioners in the police force.

Front Street in the first decade of the twentieth century. The cottages on the left were known as Jessamine Cottages and on the right can be seen the entrance to Wood Street.

WILLIAM HAMMOND,
FRONT STREET, ARNOLD,
Furniture and General Dealer,

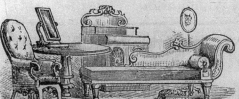

Sofas, Chairs, Clocks,

BEDSTEADS IN WOOD & IRON,

Drawers, Tables, Looking Glasses, Pier Glasses,

MATTRESSES & BEDS OF ALL DESCRIPTIONS.

Oil Paintings, Water-Drawings, Oleographs, Chromos, Prints.

All kinds of Framing done on the Premises.

WOOD AND WICKER PERAMBULATORS

Blankets, Carpets, and Rugs. Mats and Brushes. Woollen and Cotton Hosiery. Plain and Fancy Stationery.

A typical advertisement for a local business in 1875.

Blasherwicks on Front Street was the general smithy; the forge was at the rear. It is seen here in 1958.

Outside the Horse and Jockey inn, Front Street, in 1880. The driver of the coach is Tom Bailey, with his daughters on either side and Ted Bailey at the back.

In the 1970s the first of the hypermarkets arrived. Several properties of historical interest were demolished to make way for this one on Front Street, now Asda; it is seen here in 1978.

Moira House was built as a country residence for Lord Moira, a former Viceroy of India, in the eighteenth century. In 1865 Mr Allen occupied it and from this date it was known as the Doctor's House, until its demolition to make way for the superstore.

Left: Shentall's shop in the 1980s.
Right: Rowbottom's shop, before 1985. The business was founded in 1908.

Tom Turner's ironmongery in around 1965. The firm was founded in 1911; it moved across the road when the street was redeveloped, but did not survive long afterwards.

A well-known shop on Front Street, next to the old tram terminus.

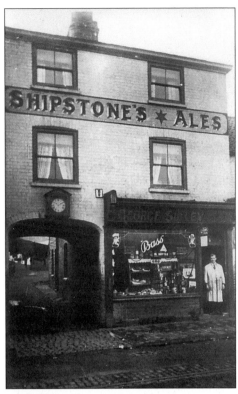

Arnold Working Men's Club members. During the General Strike of 1926 some of the members worked as soup kitchen volunteers, helping to feed the striking – and therefore unpaid – workers. Mr Impey (on the left, without a hat) was in charge of this group.

In 1894 members of the Arnold Working Men's Club won the Nottingham to Skegness cycle race.

153 Front Street, Arnold.

M. Wildgust's drapers shop at 153 Front Street was a highly respected shop.

One of the few thoroughfares between Front Street and High Street was Wellington Street, seen here in 1960. A car park is now on the site.

When the old library ceased to exist these new premises were built on the west side of Front Street. The building also accommodates swimming baths and a concert hall.

Top of the Town, *c.* 1930. This shows the tram terminus and on the right is Coppice Road, scene of the temporary market. For many years there was a notice on the wall advertising it. The shops behind were demolished and replaced by flats.

Five
Top of Town to Dorket Head

St Mary's parish church from the air in 1960. The top of the town was the site of the original settlement in Arnold, of which the parish church was the focal point. The earliest known record pertaining to a church here dates from 1176 and refers to a marriage. There was a village cross at the junction of Church Street and Calverton Road up to 1593. The church was added to from time to time, notably in 1315, 1349, 1450 and 1868-1871. The church has six bells and contains a sepulchre. As the village grew southwards and non-conformism spread, the church's influence diminished, but it is still a vital part of the community.

In the 1870s large factories appeared in the town and were to last a hundred years before progress made them obsolete. One was Clarkes on Coppice Road, shown here in 1946.

Clarkes' workforce, again in 1946. Recently the premises closed and were demolished to make way for more houses.

Like most firms, Clarkes arranged outings for employees. This is a typical photographic memento, taken at the beginning of a trip, before workers set off to enjoy themselves.

Further up Coppice Road stood Providence Place. It seems odd that houses should have been built in such an isolated spot.

The corner of Coppice Road and Church Street in 1955. This is the start of the old village, but these nineteenth-century dwellings were to disappear, to be replaced by flats.

Church Street, west side. The Robin Hood and Little John pub was known in 1765. For some unknown reason the 'Little John' part of the name was omitted for many years. On the left was Kelks Yard and the narrow thoroughfare, Cross Street.

Number 15 Church Street was built in around 1780 on the site of the old manor house. Occupied for a number of years by the medical profession, it is now in private hands. At the right-hand boundary of the manorial land there used to be a row of cottages, named Smithy Row.

The east side of Church Street, at the junction with Coppice Road. The Plough and Harrow can just be seen to the left. There was a pub on this site from at least 1832, and this building dated from 1885. It closed in 1952 and the area was cleared to make way for a block of flats.

The south side of St Mary's church, from a drawing dating from before 1870. This shows the condition of the church's fabric before restoration. The walls were leaning outwards so that at the top they were two feet off vertical, and the ends of the church were split from top to bottom, giving grave concern as to its fate. The niche above the door used to contain a figure of the Saint in honour of its dedication. To the left it is believed there is a mass grave containing the bodies of mill children, but how many is unknown.

A similar view from the 1990s. The new south porch was erected in 1924.

St Mary's church, late nineteenth century. The parish was never a wealthy living and in the second half of the nineteenth century its structure was in such a hazardous condition it required extensive repairs if was to survive. This photograph shows the general state of the stonework at that time.

The interior of the church in Edwardian times, showing the east window which was installed in 1868. The two levels of the floor are rather difficult to make out in the dim light. A rood screen was added later.

While St Mary's was undergoing restoration, the congregation used this temporary building for its devotions. It was replaced by a centre for many events, both religious and social, after the restoration in 1957/58.

In 1957 it was found that a valuable seam of coal lay beneath the church and negotiations were made to place the church on a concrete raft so that the coal could be reached. This event is now commemorated in this showcase inside the church.

The north side of the church, *c.* 1910. This aspect is said to be the oldest part of the building. For many years a story existed that a cannon ball was lodged in the tower, which was raised in 1630 and rebuilt in 1868, but examination has proved it to be the end of a supporting beam.

The 'Top' Recreation Ground, just north of the church's original graveyard, holds many happy memories for the older generation. This football match took place in 1945.

Coal was mined in the adjacent parishes giving work to many local people, and Scattergoods coal merchants were very well known. In the background of this 1993 photograph is the Manor House.

Behind Scattergoods stands a large building known as the Manor House. When the original manor (15 Church Street) was demolished, a new one was built here and remained until the land and property were bought by a Mr Nix in the 1920s. While constructing its replacement in 1929 he purchased one of the windows of the Council House in Nottingham and installed it in the 'new' manor. It is still there today, showing the city's old coat of arms. Today the Manor House is a home for the elderly.

The Congregationalists settled in Calverton Road in 1871, their early building being the one on the extreme right of this photograph. Eventually it was replaced by the larger building at the rear. This view from 1949 shows the brick air-raid shelter between the two churches, a chilling reminder of the Second World War.

An early Whit Tuesday parade from the church along Calverton Road.

Waterloo Cottages were believed to have been built and named to commemorate the great battle in 1815. They are now just a memory.

The Seven Stars inn was established in 1805 at what was then the centre of the village. It is seen here shortly before its closure in 1969, after which it was demolished to make way for housing.

Another view of the Seven
Stars inn, late 1960s.

Calverton Road School
(below) was the first school
in the area for the education
of the masses and was opened
in 1860. The population later
outgrew the school and it lay
empty for a while, until the
rooms on the right were
removed and it was reopened
as a community centre.
Recently it has been used as
the mission centre of a new
faith in the area – the New
Wine Family Church, which
is related to New Frontiers
International and the
Evangelical Alliance.

The Calverton Road and Surgeys Lane junction in 1925. The old Congregational church can be seen on the left, while Calverton Road is in the centre, leading up to Dorket Head where the Roman distribution camp was sited. On the right is Surgeys Lane. The cottages at the top were grandly called Queen Street but locally known as 'Pig Tod Alley'.

The same junction today, having been modernized.

Scrumping on Surgeys Lane, *c.* 1930.

A troup of Boy Scouts, possibly from the Top of Town. Can anyone identify them and the date of the photograph?

A forgotten way of rural life at Dorket Head Farm, 1914.

Ramsdale House, Dorket Head. The house was erected in 1907 by the Seely family on the site of the Roman encampment which, at 521ft above sea level, is one of the highest points in the area. During the Second World War it was used by the Nottingham High School for Girls as a safer alternative to their city centre location. It was bought by Nottinghamshire County Council in 1951. It was used as a hospital for some years but has recently been sold for demolition and possible development as a detention centre for young offenders.

PARLIAMENTARY ELECTION, 1900.
RUSHCLIFFE DIVISION.

Public Meeting

In support of JOHN

ROBINSON,

Esq., will be held at

Arnold,

IN THE

British School, Front St.,

ON

Monday, 8th October, 1900.

At 8 o'clock, p.m.

F. G. BANBURY, Esq., M.P.
will address the Meeting.

All Electors Cordially Invited.

VOTE FOR

John Robinson

AND THE HONOUR AND SAFETY OF THE EMPIRE.

Printed and Published by Harris, Shaw & Co., Middle Pavement, Nottingham.

A poster supporting the campaign of John Robinson at the General Election of 1900, which was won by the Conservatives.

Time, Gentlemen, Please: last orders at the Plough and Harrow inn, 1952.

Acknowledgements

I would like to thank the following for their help:

Mrs I Dalby, Mrs E. Johnson, Mrs M. Smith of Daybrook and Mrs R. Staddon from Woodthorpe for typing and correcting the work; Revd A. Clarke, Messrs G. Jackson, J. Jackson, P. Leitch and E. Woodhouse, all of Arnold; A. Ingall of Woodthorpe, J. Tanner of Mapperley, D. Humphreys of Nottingham, E. Gasson of Bramcote Moor, T. Fry of Sherwood and D. Ottewell of Eaking; last, but not least, my family for their interest and support. I dedicate this work recording the town's momentous changes as the new Millennium dawns, to them.